The Face I Desire

Selected Poems

Renuka Raghavan

Nixes Mate Books
Allston, Massachusetts

Copyright © 2019 Renuka Raghavan

Book design by d'Entremont
Cover photograph by

All rights reserved. This book or any portion thereof may not be reproduced or used in any manner whatsoever without the express written permission of the publisher except for the use of brief quotations in a book review or scholarly journal.

ISBN 978-1-949279-20-7

Nixes Mate Books
POBox 1179
Allston, MA 02134
nixesmate.pub/books

To my father, who hated poems.
::looking up, waving hello, "Miss you, Pop!"::

To Vijay, my heart,
To Riya and Raj, thanks for leaving me alone
when I write.

You three are my everything.

Contents

I. Ordering

In Search Of	4
A Storm Among Many	6
Without a Place	8
Tea(rs)	10
Stevie Knows My Secret	11
#WhatTheLove	12
Death Song for Iphigenia	13
Good Ones	15
Diorama	17
Mahākālī	19
Post-Op Wishes	21
What Remains	23
Aurora Borealis Reviews	25

II. Form

On Parade	28
(Re)incarnation	29
Grand Finale	30
The Big Bang	32
Witness Dawn	33
Scavengers	34

A Prayer for Mumtaz	35
Qutb Minar, Delhi, India	36
The Heaven We Want	38
Patchouli & Sandalwood	39
Moonlight Momentum	41
The Fisherman's Tune	42
Ride or Die	43
Testimony of Fears	44

III. Aftereffect

Clamor	46
Trusted Confidant	47
108	48
Many Little Suns	50
To My Father, Like the Sea	51
Week of Diagnosis	52
Imagined Correspondence	54
Redemption	56
Battleship	58
In the Yellow	60
When the Flames of the Pyre Die Out	62
Corvid Behavior	64

The Face I Desire

Selected Poems

"Beauty is not a means,
not a way of furthering a thing in the world.
It is a result; it belongs to ordering, to form, to aftereffect."
— Eudora Welty

I. Ordering

In Search Of

At the age of nine,
she saw him sitting on a lone playground swing.
When it was her turn on the swing,
she felt the electric charge of novelty with
his hands thrusting at her back,
but she was so very innocent about it all.

At fourteen, she saw him again.
He was different, but not different, too.
They climbed the giant oak
that now stood at the edge of the playground,
settling high upon adjacent branches,
kissing with tongues for the first time,
trying to remain innocent about it all.

At twenty-two, she went in search of herself,
traveling to lands she'd only visited in books.
When the stranger approached from behind,
she fought in his grip.
For that, he took from her more than money,
and there was nothing innocent about it all.

At thirty-three, she took warmth under the sun,
having moved to a city that was rarely
under the darkness of clouds.
But whenever she passed a playground,
her pace slowed; her eyes scanned.
She searched, always, dying to remember
what it was like to be innocent.

A Storm Among Many

With dust on the migrant flag,
my fingers write what I cannot say,
these salivating syllables drip from my tongue,

How heavy a load can one carry on her back?
One language lost, another gained, another remembered,

Like the memory of the stone temple
along the banks of the Pawana River,
or the one high upon the hill,

Now, all that's left is my writing hand
smeared with ink, calloused where the pen
rests on the side of my finger,
torn fragments of sepia-toned faces swirl into
a violent wind threatening to take me in.

I am a brown child, pinkish cheeks,
hands full of rapidly melting Cadbury's
stolen from the back of Aji's kitchen cupboard.

In my next life I am a pregnant woman
daring to cross the border without water,
the stains of my soiled skirt whirl into blood-grazed skies,
and all the shrieking rifts of the storm.

Without a Place

The mens-only room at the night shelter
had no space for personal epiphanies.
Like metal tongued by a torch's fire,
these men welded into one,
their dreams fated by auspicious disasters,
blackened flesh, earned cotton,
sedulous odors, their smug seed.

The women sat on park benches
calling out to pigeons by name,
whispering to each other like a steady drizzle,
making obscure prophecies,
lost in a haze as if searching
for something they had vomited up
that never returned back to the earth.

Together, they shiver like January nights,
trailing their life's possessions behind them
in a dreamless sleep around Dupont Circle,
sharing their stories.
A tale for each wrinkle of skin.
A caution for each scar.
Their stories still glow around dark corners,
like cat eyes, like Gatsby's green light, afire.

Tea(rs)

You would've liked the Autumn up here,
she thought silently.
Staring out the window, she sipped the hot brew.
What other experiences did we miss out on?
Each fallen teardrop salted her chamomile,
making it dense as an ocean.
Fingers caressed the gold band,
inscription memorized long ago:
I take thee,
with love.
Always.

Stevie Knows My Secret

Stevie Ray Vaughan, bronzed and weathered,
looked on as I jogged towards the young girl
wandering the red dusty trail,
flanking the lake that had once been a river.
She paused and stared at the still water
until my rapid volley of steps gave her a start.

We made brief, solid eye contact, as Axl Rose
crooned in my ears begging me not to cry tonight.
Desperate to see the next quarter mile marker
so I could ease my burning shins, I ran faster.

I think she might have smiled at me, that young girl,
who, I wish I'd known then, was moments away
from being famous.

Her cute, placid picture was plastered
on every television screen in the county
after she jumped off the interstate overpass,
ending her life and that of a truck driver's,
whose ill fate was sadly tied to hers.
After that, Stevie's beguiling charm was gone,
replaced by his keen, perceptive gaze that bore into me.

#WhatTheLove

He declared his love
was as strong as
the Hoover Dam,
plated in titanium,
covered with diamond dust.
This, I reminded him
when he kissed
my lips,
caressed
my body,
and breathed
her name.
The love is
still there,
he assured.
Sadly, he
had a surplus,
and an eager need
to share.

Death Song for Iphigenia

fragile   lifeless
he beckons her   a puppet
stuffed in blood   used
pale white lilies
of her face and breast collect
anointed tears of delight
she has arrived at the cold
shores of Aulis
on this
the day of her union to Achilles
upon his smile
her heart
beat between her legs
at the altar   the cool sting of metal
absent from her hand
instead
felt across her throat.

fragile   lifeless
with every ounce spilled out of her
she looked into her father's eyes
grieving

without prejudice
overcast by the dark clouds
that minute of mourning
cleared
all too soon
with the return of the wind
the silent blessing onward

she
whose name was born
of strength
finds herself too weak
the graying of her skin
olive wreaths and Charon's obol
her sight fixed on an Olympus
that feels too high to ascend

Good Ones

She's wearing a pink chiffon hijab,
picking out a watermelon and
talking to someone via Bluetooth.

A tiny cherub face peeks at me from
around his mother's waist.
I wave and whisper, Hello.
He grins, timid and unsure.
He temporarily disappears
back into his mother's gauzy folds.

She moves on to the cantaloupes,
as I pick up a watermelon and tap on it
with my ear against the hard rind,
just like my mother taught me.
An old man pushes his cart up to me and says,
Looks like you know how to pick out the good ones.

The little boy steps out again,
this time openly laughing at my
watermelon choosing process.
So I laugh too.

He points his fingers, thumb in the air,
index finger extended toward me.
Pew, pew, pew, soft boyish
sounds imitate.
I drop my watermelon into
the cart with exaggeration,
feigning a wounded hit.
He laughs, triumphant.

The old man says,
They really start training them young, don't they?
He'll get big and blow shit up for Allah like they do.
I wouldn't encourage him, if I were you.

The mother hears and smacks her son,
admonishing his behavior.
The cherub weeps as he's dragged out of the store
by his angered, humiliated mother.
Their cart with a watermelon and two cantaloupes,
left unattended.

It's too bad you can't spot the good ones,
I want to say to the old man,
but he's moved on.
I watch as he digs through a pile of greens to find
the best-looking spinach.

Diorama

Mrs. Miller asked with bored eyes for us to pick a country.
Any country. Create a 3-D diorama.
India, not for my heritage,
because I remember when Daddy watched TV last
night:
Breaking News: Earthquake hits Northern India.
Nearly 2,000 dead, more than 300,000
missing, injured, displaced.

I paper mâchéd a house inside an old shoebox
out of thick black construction paper,
somewhere along the foothills of the Himalayas,
with snow-capped peaks pasted for background.
The walls of the house shook,
floors torn apart, upturned furniture littered the inside,
like when Daddy used to play dollhouse
with me but his hand was too big to fit the tiny rooms.

You can't tell anything is wrong, said Mrs. Miller,
the house looks like any other. But I knew.
I knew you have to walk to the yard out back,
so I showed her the gnarled swing set,

the plastic tricycle, going through
the bottom of the shoebox,
swallowed by earth,
the wooden sandbox blown asunder.

Mahākālī

They dated for weeks before
a bed was shared.
He promised to anticipate her every desire,
only to be usurped
as the more experienced lover.
He watched her in awe,
wondering if he'd made a mistake,
regretting the warnings, he left unheeded:
"Don't date an artist, bro.
They're maniacal, crazy.
Too tired from battling their demons,
to live normal."
When they were finished,
he crept under the duvet,
unable to stop shaking
in the aftermath.
She took a seat behind her easel,
nude and inspired.
Her dark, bare thighs, her palette,
lean sinewy fingers, her brushes.
The Dark Goddess she painted
radiated beauty and quiet rage

as she slayed the cowardly demon,
collapsing him into the wet,
trampled grass.

Post-Op Wishes

Maybe he'll have a name like Jax or Finn.
Damon or Reid.
Beckett or Axel.

Maybe he'll look just as good wearing a leather jacket
as he would in a business suit.
He'll have book smarts and street smarts,
be devastatingly handsome, and
make all bad boys wish they could be him.

Maybe he'll have dark curly hair.
Not too short, not too long,
just the exact length that I can grab on to
or sift my fingers through when he holds me tight
as we slow dance to Etta James or Eric Clapton.

Maybe he'll have a hot car. A shiny red roadster
we'd take for a joyride in the middle of a summer day
with the top down.

Maybe he'll be a couple of years younger than me.
Oh, what the hell, a good ten years younger than me.

Maybe, just for kicks, he'll be the type
who bakes a cheesecake for me.
Not because it was my birthday or an anniversary,
but just because it was a Wednesday.

Maybe, when we make love for the first time,
he'll ignore my missing body parts.
He'll caress me and touch me just for pleasure,
not for pity.
And when he reaches the dual flower tattoos
inked on my flattened chest,
he'll ignore the scars behind them
and trace each petal with ardent hunger,
not wanting to break our contact.

Maybe he'll understand and be gentle
when I begin to cry.

Maybe. Just maybe.

What Remains

she stirs the stew
untroubled by the dark clouds
encroaching outside the kitchen window
he arrives home
a kiss on the cheek before
retiring to the respite of his study
a fat cigar
two fingers of Scotch
his faithful companions

the girls fall asleep
dreaming of a bunny
wearing a jacket of blue
they fill the hours of her day with commotion
soon to be replaced
with the silence of their absence
once they're grown

she remembers the cool dry soil of her homeland
each russet grain she'd sift through her fingers
before it cascaded back to the Earth in the breeze
an almost forgotten vestige

of long-ago years
full of mirth
bliss
that land long gone now
left behind to live in a giant box
pieced together with
shingles, hardwoods, stones

in the quiet end of day
the cleaning remains
the laundry remains
the loneliness remains

Aurora Borealis Reviews
a found poem

Underwhelming
Lights didn't put on a show, as promised
Too fucking cold, barely saw anything

Our tour guide was an idiot,
had us looking in the southern direction
for the Northern Lights

Buyers beware: You need clear skies
No one said seeing the Aurora was weather-dependent
Trip sucked, o stars (see what I did there?)

What a disgrace
It took nearly four hours
The most boring night of my life

Instead of looking for the Northern Lights,
we had to go looking for a lost passenger
from our tour bus

Save money and explore something else
Now I know why they call it
hunting for the Aurora Borealis
Honestly, y'all might have better luck
hunting for Bigfoot

No pictures, no lights, no refund
Just a green smudge. What's the big deal?
Best night ever: no Aurora, but I swear I saw a UFO!

II. Form

On Parade

A voice breathed down his neck,
        one whose tune he was forced to dance.
Despite the heavy of the day, he's pushed out,
bare feet on scorched cement, tattered clothes,
        permanently stained like his dream to
walk without aide.

People pass, each staring through him
        with infinite blankness,
ignoring his plea and outstretched hand.

He sees a friend peddling across the street,
        while another is passed out cold
behind the bus stall. He doesn't bat an eye,
continuing on, knowing he was only one hour
into his minimum eight for the day.

God, give him a fucking medal.
Your most beautiful crippled son,
his brothers and sisters,
        all on parade.

(Re)incarnation

Because a colossal arm of hubris
beheaded a body fleshed together
with turmeric and clay,

nursed not at his mother's bosom
but with hands and breath –
splenetic Destroyer of Evil,

the pale of his blue skin, fire of his third eye –
cowered to a mother's sorrow.

Lugubrious chants precede

rumors of a dead elephant in the North,
his not-yet decayed carcass starfished
across forgotten rubble.

Legend is (re)born

with his head now appended onto that jaundiced figure,
several gods pose behind him for scale.

Grand Finale

I dreamt of you last night.
We were standing on a giant satellite,
the size of a yellow school bus.
How did we get here, you asked?
It was always the plan, I answered.
We've been preparing ourselves
for the past ten years.
We embraced,
our bodies locked. We were
buoyant and feather light, tethered
only to each other and the
rocketing satellite.
The vast universe shining behind us,
was the canvas we painted
in radiant golds and silvers,
en route to our destination.
We stood side by side,
hand in hand,
watching particles and rings fly by
as we barreled into Saturn's glowing heart.
On this, Cassini's grand finale,
we can be as we want, my love,

knowing full well we will
never again touch the ground.

The Big Bang
for my Vijay

Heavy in our love
we lay cheek leaning on cheek, whispering
to each other of all the things that came
to our mind,
      we spoke, oh
      we spoke of it all,
our hopes,
our fears,
your arm entwined tightly with mine,
the hours of night passed as
      we spoke, oh
      we spoke of it all
without filters,
without hesitation,
with the candor of a child,
unbeknownst to us that our whole
universe was there, inside me, becoming.

Witness Dawn

Watching the trees arise –
sunlight kissing their canopies
like a mother
waking her children out of night –
awareness envelopes my surroundings,
this house, its people,
the dog, her legs twitching in final dreams,

fugitive as crimson,
my brief walk to the damp oak –
cup of black tea in hand, steam speaking
its ephemeral language into the air –
I sit on the bench dedicated to you,
stare up at the under-heavens,
marveling at unfinished business,
as it keeps bluing into the morning.

Scavengers

That ghazal recitation was his last outburst of color. He'd slash a word here and there, replace it with one of his own, a linguistic swordsman, a lone hero, waging war on stupefying boredom, defending the lost cause of verse. He was our mill into whose hoppers the grains of empty hours poured, and there, within his cogs, bloomed the fragrant aroma of the spoken words of his Motherland. We tasted his words with fervent hunger, greedily savoring each spoken syllable like a juicy morsel, until we were full. An outcast by choice, he withdrew into himself, so that the more we focused on him, the less we saw. The once blissfully tranquil sky-blue walls of his home were now thickening, graying, storming into the monotony of his acrid dialogue. Eventually his wish was fulfilled. He was forgotten.

his mind left bereft
like bones after a heartless
kill – we scavenge on

A Prayer for Mumtaz

In trepidatious script he penned a prayer
for his young Queen,
a reluctant widower, an absent father, a fallen ruler.
On the parchment the size of his palm, he added:
>I stare at the pale moon face,
>for she glows without inhibition,
>and yet my heart remains dark.
>It is your light I seek, it is your face I desire.

Between 1612 and 1631,
he remembered those days they lived in love,
picking wild flowers along the lush,
fertile banks of the Yamuna.

Qutb Minar
Delhi, India

The
lone
minaret
among a
field of ruins,
stands tall before a
pale blue Delhi sky.
A Sufi saint of another time
climbs each spiraling step
of three hundred seventy-nine
to offer prayers –
request blessings,
      seek forgiveness,
                    reach enlightenment.
His footsteps like his prayers,
echo around each bend,
through every expanse of red stone
ascending to the heavens,
descending to Earth,
      step after step,
           salah after salah,

      century after century.
At his last prayer,
I wonder if the Sufi saint
was journeying upward or down?

The Heaven We Want

The jagged arch of the Dipper's handle
beckons my hold.
This celestial sauce pot tilting high above me,
threatens to pour and pepper the heavens
in luminescent wonder.

Down below, beyond my sight, phantom fingers
plucked the strings of a phantom violin,
harmonizing despondent chords
with each passing breeze.

Elsewhere still – in cathedrals, mosques,
temples divine – a colloquy of souls await to
pray.

Billions of light-years from us,
the beginning of another species is underway.
What good does it do to pray for a heaven?
What good does it do to pray for a heaven,
if you don't take a moment to marvel the stars?

Patchouli & Sandalwood

The dirt path winding
into the woods was
as inviting as the temple
we had just left.

A house stood there,
forest ferns and greedy ivy
clutching onto gray stone.

A primrose garden off
to the side shepherded us
to a stream, loud in a stone-lain bed.

The Swami's wife, dressed in a simple
purple cotton sari, silver hair
braided down her back, welcomed us inside.

Chandana served us steaming chais
in steel tumblers, mine too hot
for me to hold.

She spoke of seclusion, sang us
hymns of loyalty, one thought after another
weaving her tapestry of faith before us.

No one has ever called this place
beautiful before, she laughed.
When we said our goodbyes, my hand lingered

on the arm of a woman who lived
up to her name, steeping us in a world
of patchouli and sandalwood.

Moonlight Momentum

You can see the moon's brightness,
illuminating the under-heavens,
her round radiance, suspended in a void,
far, far below her, steep mountain paths,
some treacherous and narrow,
over boulders, across bridges and lichens of green,
the moon's face finally rests on a deep pool,
her clinquant reflection.

The Fisherman's Tune

With no wind today on the Yamuna,
the water is too quiet and gray.
With no ripples or influx of movement,
all around the embankment, light floats in the air
over acres of smooth, rivering hematite.

An eager fisherman wants to break the solitude.
On a laborer's high, with the possibility of feeding
his family tonight,
he heaves his nets into the water,
whistling "Greensleeves" into the mist.

The music raises light to the sky,
as if a giant hovering over the distant green glen,
crooning to the diminishing moon,
ushers in the proxigean spring tide.

A blind river dolphin breaks
the crystalline surface of the water,
leaping into the air, dancing to the fisherman's tune.

Ride or Die

By the river's edge,
a tremendous grove of trees
huddle together in a cluster,
like whispering mothers
standing apart from the others
in a schoolyard.

Many with limbs missing or torn,
scarred by blades of relentless axes,
frost stripping their shawls of yellowing leaves,
battered by wind and waves,
their roots withering little by little,
wrecked and broken beyond belief,

they stand,
collectively,
– this is how survivors fare.

Testimony of Fears

When they met to honor the friend who had left this world for the next, they wielded politics like Excalibur and offensive gossip like a shield. They took women with ardent greed, like peaches shaken down from an untimely, but generous tree. The blemished autumn moon watched scum ring around their collars. Fate rested in their hands, no one else's. Three days before, the aneurysm ruptured and their friend dropped dead, out cold from their lives. And these men, fighting their fears, desperate to hide from their hearts what their tongues pushed out, cauterized their wounds with whiskey and lies.

III. Aftereffect

Clamor

Then he died – to the day –
fifty-seven years after his birth.
Nearly nothing interrupted
that December's gray.
Meager chills, bitter or brave,
or black, persisted.
His chest ached with every
draw of breath. This man –
vulnerable in his dying perfection –
slept, alas.
Then each year – on his deathday –
something within me stirs, longing
to say: If you stand facing
              the wind, eyes closed, you can
              hear the clamor abate.
To pray: Hai Bhagwan. *
To whisper: Hide.

*Hai Bhagwan: Hindi phrase meaning "Oh, God," used here, as if reciting a prayer.

Trusted Confidant

When I opened the door and peeked outside,
I saw them there, settled in a patch of green grass,
in the far corner of the yard. The little boy seated,
legs extended before him, speaking in abundant whispers
to his companion lying silent next to him.

My presence, becoming known,
made him hush his sweet breath,
embarrassed for me, the way adults stand –
hands on hips, brows furrowed –
as if all imagination was lost in the world,
as if the conversation had ended before I arrived.

I relished the sight before me, having glimpsed
a tender moment between two delicate souls.
I liked the sounds of his private thoughts
voiced with tenacious ardency.
I only wish I had been more cautious,
perhaps sat before the window – opened just a crack –
to eavesdrop unknown and allow
a little boy and his dog to converse in peace.

108

108 beads
108 chants
108 times

A small corner of our already
small apartment kitchen,
was my mother's home temple.
She prayed with her whole body
to bronze and silver deities every morning.

She crossed her legs, closed her eyes,
bowed her head, and poured all thought
into this sacred ritual.

Her rough, calloused hands that
never hesitated to confiscate my Walkman,
or tear through my rough ebony curls
with a fine-toothed comb,
now washed the Elephant God
with milk and water, delicately cleaning
each crevice. His obedient, devout disciple.
Lucky bastard.

Before it was all done, she'd settle with a
tattered prayer book in one hand,
a rudraksha mala in the other,
reciting hymns and mantras.

108 beads
108 chants
108 times

With each whispered beat,
she erased all those moments in her life
that caused an aging woman
to prostrate herself on the kitchen floor.

Many Little Suns

I lay on the lush green of the Common
watching you traipse through the knee-deep
water of a cement pond, splashing and kicking,

each molecule of water momentarily suspended,
absorbing the light of day
and glowing like many little suns.

You stand tall, swallowing the clouds,
stomping through the river,
then the woods veined with meandering
chestnut paths.

This was a place where I could have lain forever,
like a resting slug, like a forgotten twig,
like an aging stone.

To My Father, Like the Sea

I settle into the parasail harness
blinded by the glare of the sun
on the clear water below,
you shouting words of support,
from the pier behind me –
a sweet memory I dare not let go.

If memories had a scent, this would be
sea foam and sunlight,
in the middle of a Caribbean summer,
and your musky cologne enveloping me,
easing my quivering shoulders.

You did it, you did it, you said,
overcoming my fear of height,
on the cusp of womanhood,
these days of togetherness of which you cling,
unable to stop time.

Is it a wonder why we both love the sea?
Is it a wonder how we mirror each other?
Like father, like daughter,
this endless, endless water.

Week of Diagnosis

The rotting rabbit in the corner of the yard
was difficult to ignore on Sunday morning.

Mom's diagnosis was given on Monday
afternoon: clinical depression,
as if we didn't already know.

By Tuesday, the stench of the carcass
wafted through the kitchen window,
causing me to stop rinsing dishes.

Curiosity had built up, so on Wednesday,
I had to go look again.

Fat black flies were buzzing around its face.
Plump maggots ate away the torso and legs.

Crows picked at its hindquarters,
or what was left of it.
Mom came for lunch the next afternoon.

We sat with glasses of sweet tea,
our hands soaked with condensation,
as I silently prayed to the gods of serotonin.

Did you take the new meds, Ma?
She smiled serenely,
shielding her face from the sun,
from me, from herself.

We should plant the azaleas in that corner,
she said, pointing to the bunny's boneyard.
I nodded, *Let's give it another week or so*.

By Friday, the corpse looked like an empty shell,
its hollowed ribcage and skull reminding
me of the sperm whale remains
lying on the ocean floor that I saw on *Blue Planet*.

When I dug the hole for the azaleas,
I chucked the rabbit's remains to the very bottom.

Imagined Correspondence

If you only knew how many letters I've written you.
Mostly in my head, when I travel
over one continent to another, pretending to be lost.

Once, the words made it all the way onto paper.
But it contained nothing of importance:
How cold I felt as I walked the dog,
up and back again on the Upper Falls greenbelt,
even in those warm days,
that biting absence of your presence
chilling me to the bone,
just as you predicted.

I wrote of the state of trees
along the lash of a blown ravine,
how hoarfrost worked its spiky tendrils,
determined to cover nearly all things knee-high;
iced branches threaded to one another
in frozen embroidery.

When, last fall, an orb-weaver spun his web
above the front porch
dropping line after line of silk Ys.
How at the center, he took rest,
curving inward to catch his breath,
the way I dream you are still here to catch yours.

How in Iceland hundreds of puffins nest on cliffsides,
yet each bird knows exactly which nook is his.
The Icelandic have a phrase for this, *stað fyrir allt*,
a place for everything, everything in its place
and I am reminded of all creatures in their homes
under this Arctic winter sun.

Redemption

Three days after that kid's funeral,
the old man living in the purple Victorian
across the street,
who is often laughed at by us neighbors
for standing out in front of his home
in tattered pajama bottoms
yelling at God,
and how he only ever talks to women
on days ending in zero,
stood before me on my front porch.

Plowing through the loud thrum
of traffic and guilt,
rubbing my swollen belly
where a tiny arm or leg
was determined to punch through,
I ask him what he wants and why he's at my door.

What he says, around his cigarette
while pointing to the corner of our street,
where neighborhood kids cross
on their way home from school,

where there now lay flowers, pictures,
and stuffed animals of various species,
what he says is, "Don't worry. Don't worry, girl.
You'll still make a good mama."

Battleship

a pantoum

I never meant to bother you
When I asked if you'd play a game with me
I wanted you to say, Anything for you, Honeybun, but you didn't
I was seven at the time

When I asked if you'd play a game with me
You turned your nose and looked heavenwards
I was seven at the time
Don't think I didn't know

You turned your nose and looked heavenwards
Silently praying for a miracle to save you
Don't think I didn't know
With the bombing of E-4, I sank your battleship

Silently praying for a miracle to save you
You sat awkwardly, trying to hide your smile
With the bombing of E-4, I sank your battleship
But I failed in my unsportsmanlike triumph, disappointing you

You sat awkwardly, trying to hide your smile
Noting the gleam in my eye as your loss
became inevitable
but I failed in my unsportsmanlike triumph,
disappointing you
Now I fear you'd never play with me again

Noting the gleam in my eye as your loss
became inevitable
A proud, high-pitched squeal escaped my lips
Now I fear you'd never play with me again
Yet, somehow, that day became one of my fondest

A proud, high-pitched squeal escaped my lips
I wanted you to say, Anything for you, Honeybun,
but you didn't
Yet, somehow, that day became one of my fondest
I never meant to bother you

In the Yellow

One chore leads to another still
at the onset of this cool Spring day,

the dog snoring on her bed,
witch hazel blooming.

You have to pay attention
to know when a door presents itself.

In the clement sun-pollinating morning,
the kitchen bursts into flame,

the portal opens and I step
back into another day.

Not the mere memory of it,
but the time itself, that easy light and air,

my body still mine,
but years before my womb carried another.

The depleted skin of lemons and limes,
squeezed dry, lay in a heap

as my father's brittle hand sprinkled another
spoon of sugar into a glass pitcher.

My mother hummed
as she arranged her herbs and spices,

mustard seeds, turmeric, bay leaves,
coriander and saffron,

all lined in identical jars
below the windowsill.

I return reluctantly,
or perhaps not at all.

When the Flames of the Pyre Die Out

We collect the
heaps of ash,
the dry, arid
stench of marrow
tattooed onto our
olfactory senses,
fighting with the
sweet aroma of
surrounding
jasmine and peony,
grass and sandalwood.
Our canvas is
the calm river,
a gentle sway
invites us to
her banks on
this bright day.
A koel expels
his sharp cries,
then flies off
to find a
mate.

Soundless intervals
amidst unknown
incantations invoke dead
spirits of our
past to come
and escort the
newest departed soul
to rest.
The fragile staccato of
each spoken hymn
hushes into a
dull beat, a
soft cadence that
accompanies them to
a quiet place
beyond the blind,
eager reaches of
our longing sorrow.

Corvid Behavior

When I was younger,
Papa used to call me Tillu and read fables.
The one about a crow so thirsty and clever
he made a few drops of water reach the top of a pitcher
by adding stones, one by one – my favorite.

I was a hummingbird, one with speckled wings,
flitting from one day to the next,
relishing everything sweet before me.

Then, that year, the monsoon drowned our house,
the courtyard filled with clouds,
the veranda became a wind tunnel,
and me with my stippled wings, got caught in it.

I fell from my bed into a wonderland.
Petals paraded across blue skies,
shrouding mister sun and sister moon.
Black and white portraits with mouths torn out
spoke dactylic truths.

I couldn't find my glasses, righting myself,
squinting as much as I could without closing my eyes,
I peered into the back garden where I saw a tiny feline
curled at the foot of Papa's ghost.

Half-hidden under a palm frond,
he was collecting stones, one by one.

"The act of writing, it seems to me, makes up a shelter, allows space to what would otherwise be hidden, crossed out, mutilated. Sometimes writing can work toward a reparation, making a sheltering space for the mind. Yet it feeds off ruptures, tears in what might otherwise seem a seamless, oppressive fabric."
—*Meena Alexander*

AUTHOR'S NOTE

To Michael McInnis and Annie Pluto, I can't thank you enough for your constant advocation of writers and their work. For that, you are so very appreciated.

To Tom Daley, thank you for dispensing your wisdom and guidance for many of the pieces in this collection.

To Gloria Mindock and Karen Friedland, I cherish our friendship. Thank you for motivating me and helping me along the way.

Hey Rich Fienberg, it's true what they say – not all heroes wear capes. Thank you.

To Mrs. Sujata Pant, Mr. S. Raghavan, and Mrs. Jeyaseeli Akiahnaicker, my pillars of strength and tradition, thank you for the continuous encouragement.

ACKNOWLEDGEMENTS

The following pieces have previously been published, some in slightly different versions:

"Good Ones" in *Mom Egg Review* Vol. 17

"In Search Of" in *Constellations*, Vulnerability Vol. 8

"Grand Finale" in *Nixes Mate Review*, Spring 2018

"What Remains" in *River Poets Journal* Themed Issue: The Immigrants

"When the Flames of the Pyre Die Out," "The Big Bang," and "Many Little Suns," in *The Poets of New England Anthology* Vol. 1

"Week of Diagnosis" in *Muddy River Poetry Review* Issue #19

"Post-Op Wishes" on Spelk Fiction

"Diorama" and "Without a Place" in *Lily Poetry Review*, Winter 2018 Issue

"Aurora Borealis Reviews," "Ride or Die," "Scavengers," "Corvid Behavior," and "In the Yellow" in *Muddy River Poetry Review* Fall 2019

"Redemption" and "Testimony of Fears" on *Flash Boulevard*

"Imagined Correspondence" in a Nixes Mate broadside
"(Re)incarnation" on *Live Nude Poems*

A heartfelt thank you to the editors of these fine publications.

About the Author

Renuka Raghavan is the author of *Out of the Blue* (2017). Her poems and short fiction have been published in literary journals across the United States, with most recent work featured in *Mom Egg Review* and *Gravel Literary Magazine*. Renuka serves as the fiction book reviewer at Červená Barva Press, and is a poetry reader for Indolent Books and the Lily Poetry Review. She is also a co-founder of the Poetry Sisters Collective. Renuka writes and lives in Massachusetts with her family and beloved beagle.
Visit her at renukaraghavan.com

42° 19' 47.9" N   70° 56' 43.9" W

Nixes Mate is a navigational hazard in Boston Harbor used during the colonial period to gibbet and hang pirates and mutineers.

Nixes Mate Books features small-batch artisanal literature, created by writers who use all 26 letters of the alphabet and then some, honing their craft the time-honored way: one line at a time.

nixesmate.pub/books

www.ingramcontent.com/pod-product-compliance
Lightning Source LLC
Chambersburg PA
CBHW050618130526
44591CB00045B/2338